The Super Simple Air Fryer Cookbook

Mouth-watering and Amazing Recipes for
Busy People.
Cook in a Few Steps and Say Goodbye to
Hypertension and Hemicranias. Lose Weight
fast and Get Lean.

Tanya Hackett

Table of Contents

The information in the following pages is broadly considered a truthful and accurate account of facts and as such, any inattention, use, or misuse of the information in question by the reader will render any resulting actions solely under their purview. There are no scenarios in which the publisher or the original author of this work can be in any fashion deemed liable for any hardship or damages that may befall them after undertaking information described herein.

Additionally, the information in the following pages is intended only for informational purposes and should thus be thought of as universal. As befitting its nature, it is presented without assurance regarding its prolonged validity or interim quality. Trademarks that are mentioned are done without written consent and can in no way be considered an endorsement from the trademark holder.

Introduction

An air fryer is a relatively new kitchen appliance that has proven to be very popular among consumers. While there are many different varieties available, most air fryers share many common features. They all have heating elements that circulate hot air to cook the food. Most come with pre-programmed settings that assist users in preparing a wide variety of foods.

Air frying is a healthier style of cooking because it uses less oil than traditional deep frying methods. While it preserves the flavor and quality of the food, it reduces the amount of fat used in cooking. Air frying is a common method for "frying" foods that are primarily made with eggs and flour. These foods can be soft or crunchy to your preference by using this method.

How air fryers work

Air fryers use a blower to circulate hot air around food. The hot air heats the moisture on the food until it evaporates and creates steam. As steam builds up around the food, it creates pressure that pulls moisture from the surface of the food and pushes it away from the center, forming small bubbles. The bubbles creates a layer of air that surrounds the food and creates a crispy crust.

Choosing an air fryer

When choosing an air fryer, look for one that has good reviews for customer satisfaction. Start with the features you need, such as power, capacity size and accessories. Look for one that is easy to use. Some air fryers on the market have a built-in timer and adjustable temperature. Look for one with a funnel to catch grease, a basket that is dishwasher-safe and parts that are easy to clean.

How To Use An Air Fryer

For best results, preheat the air fryer at 400 F for 10 minutes. Preheating the air fryer allows it to reach the right temperature faster. In addition, preheating the air fryer is essential to ensure that your food won't burn.

How to cook stuff in an Air Fryer

If you don't have an air fryer yet, you can start playing with your ovens by throwing some frozen fries in there and cooking them until they are browned evenly. Depending on your oven, take a look at the temperature. You may need to increase or decrease the time.

What Foods Can You Cook In An Air Fryer?

Eggs: While you can cook eggs in an air fryer, we don't recommend it because you can't control the cooking time and temperature as precisely as with a traditional frying pan or skillet. It's much easier to get unevenly cooked eggs. You also can't toss in any sauces or seasonings and you won't get crispy, golden brown edges.

Frozen foods: Generally, frozen foods are best cooked in the conventional oven because they need to reach a certain temperature to be properly cooked. The air fryer is not capable of reaching temperatures that result in food being fully cooked.

Dehydrated Foods: Dehydrated foods require deep-frying, which is not something you can do with an air fryer. When it comes to cooking dehydrated foods, the air fryer is not the best option.

Vegetables: You can cook vegetables in an air fryer but you have to make sure that the air fryer is not set at a temperature that will burn them.

To ensure that your vegetables aren't overcooked, start the air fryer with the basket off, then toss in the veggies once the air has heated up and there are no more cold spots.

Make sure to stir the vegetables every few minutes. Cooking them in the basket is also an option, but they may stick together a little bit.

Fries: Frying fries in an air fryer is a good way to get crispy, golden-brown fries without adding lots of oil. Compared to conventional frying, air frying yields fewer calories.

To cook french fries in an air fryer, use a basket or a rack and pour in enough oil to come about halfway up the height of the fries. For best results, make sure the fries are frozen. Turn the air fryer onto 400 degrees and set it for 12 minutes. If you want them extra crispy, you can set it for 18 minutes, but they may burn a bit.

Benefits of an air fryer:

• It's one of the easiest ways to cook healthy foods. Used 4-5 times a week, it's a healthier option than frying with oil in your conventional oven or using canned foods.

• Air fryer meals are an easy way to serve tasty food that doesn't take up lots of space. Air fryers make it possible to cook three times as much food as you can in your microwave.

• Air fryers have a small footprint and you can store them away in a cabinet when not in use.

•They are versatile kitchen appliances. You can use them to cook food for lunch, dinner and snacks.

• Air fryers require little to no fussing in the kitchen. You can use them with the lid on, which means there's less washing up to do.

Honey Banana Chips

Basic Recipe

Preparation Time: 10 minutes

Cooking Time: 6 minutes

Servings: 2

Ingredients:

1. 2 bananas
2. 1 teaspoon honey
3. 1 pinch white pepper
4. ½ teaspoon olive oil

Directions:

- Peel the bananas and slice them into the chip's pieces. Then sprinkle the bananas with the honey and white pepper.
- Spray the olive oil over the bananas and mix them gently with the help of the hands.
- Preheat the air fryer to 320 F. Put the banana chips in the air fryer basket and cook for 6 minutes
- Serve the cooked banana chips immediately.
- Enjoy!

Nutrition:

Calories 126

Fat 1.6

Carbs 29.9

Protein 1.3

Ginger Apple Chips

Basic Recipe

Preparation Time: 10 minutes

Cooking Time: 10 minutes

Servings: 2

Ingredients:

1. ½ teaspoon olive oil

2. 3 apples

3. 1 pinch ground ginger

Directions:

- Peel the apples and remove the seeds. Slice the apples and sprinkle them with the ground ginger and olive oil.

- Preheat the air fryer to 400 F.

- Place the apple slices on the air fryer rack.
- Cook the apple chips for 10 minutes
- Shake the apple chips carefully after 4 minutes of cooking.
- Then chill the apple chips carefully.
- Serve the meal immediately or keep it in the paper bag in the dry place.
- Enjoy!

Nutrition:

Calories 184

Fat 1.8

Fiber 8.1

Carbs 46.3

Protein 0.9

Maple Carrot Fries

Basic Recipe

Preparation Time: 5 minutes

Cooking Time: 10 minutes

Servings: 2

Ingredients:

1. 1 cup baby carrot
2. ¼ cup maple syrup
3. 1 pinch salt
4. ½ teaspoon thyme
5. ½ teaspoon ground black pepper
6. 1 teaspoon dried oregano
7. 1 tablespoon olive oil

Directions:

- Preheat the air fryer to 410 F.
- Place the baby carrot in the air fryer basket.
- Sprinkle the baby carrot with the thyme, salt, ground black pepper, and dried oregano.
- Then spray the olive oil over the baby carrot and shake it well.
- Cook the baby carrot fries for 10 minutes
- Shake the carrot fries after 6 minutes of cooking.
- Chill the cooked meal for 5 minutes
- Enjoy!

Nutrition:

Calories 197

Fat 7.3

Carbs 34.4

Protein 0.7

Sweet Potato Fries

Basic Recipe

Preparation Time: 10 minutes

Cooking Time: 15 minutes

Servings: 2

Ingredients:

1. 2 sweet potatoes
2. 1 tablespoon coconut oil
3. 1/3 teaspoon salt
4. ½ teaspoon ground black pepper
5. ½ teaspoon onion powder

Directions:

- Preheat the air fryer to 370 F.
- Peel the sweet potatoes and cut them into the fries.
- Sprinkle the vegetables with the salt, ground black pepper, and onion powder.
- Shake the sweet potatoes and sprinkle with the coconut oil.
- Put the uncooked sweet potato fries in the air fryer basket and cook for 15 minutes
- Shake the sweet potato fries every 5 minutes
- When the sweet potato fries are cooked: let them chill gently
- Serve the meal!

Nutrition:

Calories 225

Fat 6.8

Carbs 42.1

Protein 2.6

Squid Rings

Basic Recipe

Preparation Time: 10 minutes

Cooking Time: 4 minutes

Servings: 2

Ingredients:

1. 2 squid tubes
2. 2 eggs
3. 1/3 cup flour
4. ¼ teaspoon salt
5. ½ teaspoon onion powder
6. ½ teaspoon garlic powder

Directions:

- Wash and peel the squid cubes carefully. Then slice the squid cubes into the rings.
- Beat the eggs in the bowl and whisk them.
- Then dip the squid rings in the whisked eggs.
- Combine together flour, salt, onion powder, and garlic powder. Stir the mixture with the help of the fork.
- Then coat the squid rings with the flour mixture.
- Preheat the air fryer to 400 F.
- Put the squid rings onto the air fryer rack.
- Cook the squid rings for 4 minutes
- Shake the squid rings after 3 minutes of cooking.
- When the squid rings are cooked: let them chill till the room temperature
- Enjoy!

Nutrition:

Calories 383

Fat 10.5

Carbs 17.2

Protein 55.8

Carrot Chips

Basic Recipe

Preparation Time: 10 minutes

Cooking Time: 20 minutes

Servings: 2

Ingredients:

1. 3 carrots
2. ½ teaspoon salt
3. ½ teaspoon ground black pepper
4. 1 tablespoon canola oil

Directions:

- Peel the carrot and slice into the chips.
- Then sprinkle the uncooked carrot chips with the salt, ground black pepper, and canola oil.
- Shake the carrot chips carefully.
- Preheat the air fryer to 360 F.
- Put the carrot chips in the air fryer basket.
- Shake the carrot chips in halfway.
- Check the doneness of the carrot chips while cooking.
- Chill the carrot chips and serve.
- Enjoy!

Nutrition:

Calories 101

Fat 7

Carbs 9.3

Protein 0.8

Corn Okra Bites

Basic Recipe

Preparation Time: 10 minutes

Cooking Time: 4 minutes

Servings: 2

Ingredients:

1. 4 tablespoon corn flakes, crushed
2. 9 oz okra
3. 1 egg
4. ½ teaspoon salt
5. 1 teaspoon olive oil

Directions:

- Preheat the air fryer to 400 F.
- Chop the okra roughly.
- Combine together the corn flakes and salt.
- Crack the egg into the bowl and whisk it.
- Toss the chopped okra in the whisked egg.
- Then coat the chopped okra with the corn flakes.
- Put the chopped okra in the air fryer basket and sprinkle with the olive oil.
- Cook the okra for 4 minutes
- Shake the okra after 2 minutes of cooking.
- When the okra is cooked: let it chill gently.
- Enjoy!

Nutrition:

Calories 115

Fat 4.8

Carbs 12.7

Protein 5.2

Salty Potato Chips

Basic Recipe

Preparation Time: 10 minutes

Cooking Time: 19 minutes

Servings: 2

Ingredients:

1. 3 potatoes
2. 1 tablespoon canola oil
3. ½ teaspoon salt

Directions:

- Wash the potatoes carefully and do not peel them. Slice the potatoes into the chips.
- Sprinkle the potato chips with the olive oil and salt. Mix the potatoes carefully.

- Preheat the air fryer to 400 F. Put the potato chips in the air fryer basket and cook for 19 minutes
- Shake the potato chips every 3 minutes
- When the potato chips are cooked: chill them well.
- Enjoy!

Nutrition:

Calories 282

Fat 7.3

Carbs 50.2

Protein 5.4

Corn & Beans Fries

Basic Recipe

Preparation Time: 10 minutes

Cooking Time: 10 minutes

Servings: 2

Ingredients:

1. ¼ cup corn flakes crumbs
2. 1 egg
3. 10 oz green beans
4. 1 tablespoon canola oil
5. ½ teaspoon salt
6. 1 teaspoon garlic powder

Directions:

- Preheat the air fryer to 400 F.
- Put the green beans in the bowl.
- Beat the egg in the green beans and stir carefully until homogenous.
- Then sprinkle the green beans with the salt and garlic powder.
- Shake gently.
- Then coat the green beans in the corn flakes crumbs well.
- Put the green beans in the air fryer basket in one layer.
- Cook the green beans for 7 minutes
- Shake the green beans twice during the cooking.

- When the green beans are cooked: let them chill and serve.
- Enjoy!

Nutrition:

Calories 182

Fat 9.4

Carbs 21

Protein 6.3

Sugary Apple Fritters

Basic Recipe

Preparation Time: 10 minutes

Cooking Time: 10 minutes

Servings: 2

Ingredients:

1. 2 red apples
2. 1 teaspoon sugar
3. 1 tablespoon flour
4. 1 tablespoon semolina
5. 1 teaspoon lemon juice
6. ½ teaspoon ground cinnamon
7. 1 teaspoon butter
8. 1 egg

Directions:

- Peel the apples and grate them.
- Sprinkle the grated apples with the lemon juice.
- Then add sugar, flour, semolina, and ground cinnamon.
- Mix the mixture and crack the egg.
- Mix the apple mixture carefully.
- Preheat the air fryer to 370 F.
- Toss the butter in the air fryer basket and melt it.
- When the butter is melted: make the medium fritters from the apple mixture. Use 2 spoons for this step.

- Place the fritters in the air fryer basket and cook for 6 minutes
- After this, flip the fritters to another side and cook for 2 minutes more.
- Dry the cooked fritters with the help of the paper towel and serve.
- Enjoy!

Nutrition:

Calories 207

Fat 4.6

Carbs 40.3

Protein 4.5

Oregano Onion Rings

Basic Recipe

Preparation Time: 14 minutes

Cooking Time: 10 minutes

1. **Servings:** 2
2. **Ingredients:**
3. 1 tablespoon oregano
4. 1 tablespoon flour
5. ½ teaspoon cornstarch
6. 1 egg
7. ½ teaspoon salt
8. 2 white onions, peeled
9. 1 tablespoon olive oil

Directions:

- Crack the egg into the bowl and whisk it. Combine together the flour and cornstarch in the separate bowl.
- Add oregano and salt. Shake the mixture gently. Peel the onions and slice them to get the "rings".
- Then dip the onion rings in the whisked egg. After this, coat the onion rings in the flour mixture.
- Preheat the air fryer to 365 F.
- Spray the air fryer basket with the olive oil inside. Then place the onion rings in the air fryer and cook for 8 minutes
- Shake the onion rings after 4 minutes of cooking. Let the cooked meal chill gently.
- Serve it!

Nutrition:

Calories 159

Fat 9.6

Carbs 15.5

Protein 4.6

Cinnamon Mixed Nuts

Basic Recipe

Preparation Time: 5 minutes

Cooking Time: 20 minutes

Servings: 5

Ingredients:

1. ½ cup pecans
2. ½ cup walnuts
3. ½ cup almonds
4. A pinch of cayenne pepper
5. 2 tbsp sugar
6. 2 tbsp egg whites
7. 2 tsp cinnamon

Directions

- Add the pepper, sugar, and cinnamon to a bowl and mix them well; set aside. In another bowl, mix in the pecans, walnuts, almonds, and egg whites. Add the spice mixture to the nuts and give it a good mix. Lightly grease the frying basket with cooking spray. Pour in the nuts, and cook them for 10 minutes on Air Fry function at 350 F. Stir the nuts using a wooden vessel, and cook for further for 10 minutes Pour the nuts in the bowl. Let cool.

Nutrition:

Calories 180

Fat 12g

Carbs 13g

Protein 6g

Apple & Cinnamon Chips

Basic Recipe

Preparation Time: 15 minutes

Cooking Time: 10 minutes

Servings: 2

Ingredients:

1. 1 tsp sugar
2. 1 tsp salt
3. 1 whole apple, sliced
4. ½ tsp cinnamon
5. Confectioners' sugar for serving

Directions:

- Preheat your Air Fryer to 400 F. In a bowl, mix cinnamon, salt and sugar; add the apple slices. Place the prepared apple spices in the cooking basket and cook for 10 minutes on Bake function. Dust with sugar and serve.

Nutrition:

Calories 110

Fat 0g

Carbs 27g

Protein 1g

Sesame Cabbage & Prawns Egg Roll Wraps

Basic Recipe

Preparation Time: 32 minutes

Cooking Time: 18 minutes

Servings: 4

Ingredients:

1. 2 tbsp vegetable oil
2. 1-inch piece fresh ginger, grated
3. 1 tbsp minced garlic
4. 1 carrot, cut into strips
5. ¼ cup chicken broth
6. 2 tbsp reduced-sodium soy sauce
7. 1 tbsp sugar
8. 1 cup shredded Napa cabbage
9. 1 tbsp sesame oil
10. 8 cooked prawns, minced
11. 1 egg
12. 8 egg roll wrappers

Directions

- In a skillet over high heat, heat vegetable oil, and cook ginger and garlic for 40 seconds, until fragrant. Stir in carrot and cook for another 2 minutes Pour in chicken broth, soy sauce, and sugar and bring to a boil.

- Add cabbage and let simmer until softened, for 4 minutes Remove skillet from the heat and stir in sesame oil. Let cool for 15 minutes Strain cabbage mixture, and fold in minced prawns. Whisk an egg in a small bowl. Fill each egg roll wrapper with prawn mixture, arranging the mixture just below the center of the wrapper.
- Fold the bottom part over the filling and tuck under. Fold in both sides and tightly roll up. Use the whisked egg to seal the wrapper. Place the rolls into a greased frying basket, spray with oil and cook for 12 minutes at 370 F on Air Fry function, turning once halfway through.

Nutrition:

Calories 149.3

Fat 3.5g

Carbs 20g

Protein8.8 g

Rosemary Potatoes

Basic Recipe

Preparation Time: 10 minutes

Cooking Time: 25 minutes

Servings: 2

Ingredients:

- pounds potatoes, halved
1. 2 tbsp olive oil
2. 3 garlic cloves, grated
3. 1 tbsp minced fresh rosemary
4. 1 tsp salt
5. ¼ tsp freshly ground black pepper

Directions:

1. In a bowl, mix potatoes, olive oil, garlic, rosemary, salt, and pepper, until they are well-coated. Arrange the potatoes in the basket and cook t 360 F on Air Fry function for 25 minutes, shaking twice during the cooking. Cook until crispy on the outside and tender on the inside.

Nutrition:

Calories 132

Fats: 2.5g

Carbs 18.3g

Protein 9.5g

Crunchy Mozzarella Sticks with Sweet Thai Sauce

Intermediate Recipe
Preparation Time: 2 hours
Cooking Time: 20 minutes
Servings: 2
Ingredients:

- 12 mozzarella string cheese
- 2 cups breadcrumbs
- 3 eggs
- 1 cup sweet Thai sauce
- 4 tbsp skimmed milk

Directions

1. Pour the crumbs in a bowl. Crack the eggs into another bowl and beat with the milk. One after the other, dip each cheese sticks in the egg mixture, in the crumbs, then egg mixture again and then in the crumbs again.

2. Place the coated cheese sticks on a cookie sheet and freeze for 1 to 2 hours. Preheat Air Fry function to 380 F. Arrange the sticks in the frying basket without overcrowding. Cook for 8 minutes, flipping them halfway through cooking to brown evenly. Cook in batches. Serve with a sweet Thai sauce.

Nutrition:
Calories 173

Fat 5.6g

Carbs 27g

Protein 3.3g

Chicken Soup

Preparation Time: 10 minutes

Cooking Time: 17 minutes

Servings: 4

Ingredients:

- 4chicken breasts, skinless and boneless
- 2tablespoons extra virgin olive oil
- 1 onion, peeled and chopped
- 3garlic cloves, peeled and minced
- 16ounces chunky salsa
- 29ounces canned diced tomatoes
- 29ounces chicken stock
- Salt and ground black pepper, to taste
- 2tablespoons dried parsley
- 1 teaspoon garlic powder
- 1 tablespoon onion powder
- 1 tablespoon chili powder
- 15ounces frozen corn
- 32ounces canned black beans, drained

Directions:

1. Put the air fryeron Sauté mode, add the oil, and heat it up. Put in the onion, stir, and cook 5 minutes. Add the garlic, stir, and cook for a minute.

2. Put in the chicken breasts, tomatoes, salsa, pepper, onion powder, stock, salt, garlic powder, parsley, and chili powder, stir, cover, and cook on the Soup setting for 8 minutes. Naturally release the pressure for 10 minutes, uncover the Air fryer, transfer the chicken breasts to a cutting board, shred with 2 forks, and return to pot. Add the beans and corn, Put the air fryeron Manual mode and cook for 2-3 minutes. Divide into soup bowls, and serve.

Nutrition:

Calories: 210

Protein: 26 g.

Fat: 4.4 g.

Carbs: 18 g.

Potato and Cheese Soup

Preparation Time: 10 minutes

Cooking Time: 10 minutes

Servings: 6

Ingredients:

- 6cups potatoes, cubed
- 2tablespoons butter
- ½ cup yellow onion, chopped
- 28ounces chicken stock
- Salt and ground black pepper, to taste
- 2tablespoons dried parsley
- 1/8 teaspoon red pepper flakes
- 2tablespoons cornstarch

- 2tablespoons water
- 3ounces cream cheese, cubed
- 2cups half and half
- 1 cup cheddar cheese, shredded
- 1 cup corn
- 6bacon slices, cooked and crumbled

Directions:

1. Put the air fryeron Sauté mode, add the butter and melt it. Put in the onion, stir, and cook 5 minutes.
2. Add half of the stock, salt, pepper, pepper flakes, and parsley and stir. Put the potatoes in the steamer basket, cover the Air fryer and cook on the Steam setting for 4 minutes. Naturally release the pressure, uncover the Air fryer, and transfer the potatoes to a bowl. In another bowl, mix the cornstarch with water and stir well. Put the air fryerto Manual mode, add the cornstarch slurry, cream cheese, and shredded cheese and stir well. Add the rest of the stock, corn, bacon, potatoes, half and half. Stir, bring to a simmer, ladle into bowls, and serve.

Nutrition:

Calories: 188

Protein: 9 g.

Fat: 7.14 g.

Carbs: 22 g.

Split Pea Soup

Preparation Time: 10 minutes

Cooking Time: 20 minutes

Servings: 6

Ingredients:

- 2tablespoons butter
- 1 pound chicken sausage, ground
- 1 yellow onion, peeled and chopped
- ½ cup carrots, peeled and chopped
- ½ cup celery, chopped
- 2garlic cloves, peeled and minced
- 29ounces chicken stock
- Salt and ground black pepper, to taste
- 2cups water
- 16ounces split peas, rinsed
- ½ cup half and half
- ¼ teaspoon red pepper flakes

Directions:

1. Put the air fryeron Sauté mode, add the sausage, brown it on all sides and transfer to a plate. P

49

2. ut the butter in the Air fryer and melt it. Add the celery, onions, and carrots, stir, and cook 4 minutes. Mix in the garlic, stir and cook for 1 minute. Add the water, stock, peas and pepper flakes, stir, cover and cook on the Soup setting for 10 minutes. Release the pressure, puree the mix using an immersion blender and Put the air fryeron Manual mode. Add the sausage, salt, pepper, and half and half, stir, bring to a simmer, and ladle into soup bowls.

Nutrition:

Calories: 30

Protein: 20 g.

Fat: 11 g.

Carbs: 14 g.

Corn Soup

Preparation Time: 10 minutes

Cooking Time: 15 minutes

Servings: 4

Ingredients:

- 2leeks, chopped
- 2tablespoons butter
- 2garlic cloves, peeled and minced
- 6ears of corn, cobs reserved, kernels cut off,
- 2bay leaves
- 4tarragon sprigs, chopped
- 1-quart chicken stock
- Salt and ground black pepper, to taste
- Extra virgin olive oil
- 1 tablespoon fresh chives, chopped

Directions:

1. Put the air fryeron Sauté mode, add the butter and melt it.
2. Add the leeks and garlic, stir, and cook for 4 minutes.
3. Add the corn, corn cobs, bay leaves, tarragon, and stock to cover everything, cover the Air fryer and cook on the Soup setting for 15 minutes.

4. Release the pressure, uncover the Air fryer, discard the bay leaves and corn cobs, and transfer everything to a blender. Pulse well to obtain a smooth soup, add the rest of the stock and blend again.
5. Add the salt and pepper, stir well, divide into soup bowls, and serve cold with chives and olive oil on top.

Nutrition:

Calories: 300

Protein: 13 g.

Fat: 8.3 g.

Carbs: 50 g.

Butternut Squash Soup

Preparation Time: 10 minutes

Cooking Time: 16 minutes

Servings: 6

Ingredients:

- 1½ pounds butternut squash, baked, peeled and cubed
- ½ cup green onions, chopped
- 3tablespoons butter
- ½ cup carrots, peeled and chopped
- ½ cup celery, chopped
- 29ounces chicken stock
- 1 garlic clove, peeled and minced
- ½ teaspoon Italian seasoning

- 15ounces canned diced tomatoes
- Salt and ground black pepper, to taste
- 1/8 teaspoon red pepper flakes
- 1 cup orzo, already cooked
- 1/8 teaspoon nutmeg, grated
- 1½ cup half and half
- 1 cup chicken meat, already cooked and shredded
- Green onions, chopped, for serving

Directions:

1. Put the air fryeron Sauté mode, add the butter and melt it. Add the celery, carrots, and onions, stir, and cook for 3 minutes.

2. Put in the garlic, stir, and cook for 1 minute. Add the squash, tomatoes, stock, Italian seasoning, salt, pepper, pepper flakes, and nutmeg. Stir, cover the Air fryer, and cook on the Soup setting for 10 minutes. Release the pressure, uncover, and puree everything with an immersion blender. Put the air fryeron Manual mode, add the half and half, orzo, and chicken, stir, and cook for 3 minutes. Divide the soup into bowls, sprinkle green onions on top, and serve.

Nutrition:

Calories: 130

Protein: 6 g.

Fat: 2.3 g.

Carbs: 18 g.

Beef and Rice Soup

Preparation Time: 10 minutes

Cooking Time: 15 minutes

Servings: 6

Ingredients:

- 1 pound ground beef
- 3garlic cloves, peeled and minced
- 1 yellow onion, peeled and chopped
- 1 tablespoon vegetable oil
- 1 celery stalk, chopped
- 28ounces beef stock
- 14ounces canned crushed tomatoes
- ½ cup white rice
- 12ounces spicy tomato juice
- 15ounces canned garbanzo beans, rinsed
- 1 potato, cubed
- Salt and ground black pepper, to taste
- ½ cup frozen peas
- 2carrots, peeled and sliced thin

Directions:

1. Put the air fryeron Sauté mode, add the beef, stir, cook until it browns, and transfer to a plate. Add the oil to the Air fryer and heat it up.

2. Add the celery and onion, stir, and cook for 5 minutes. Put in the garlic, stir and cook for 1 minute. Add the tomato juice, stock, tomatoes, rice, beans, carrots, potatoes, beef, salt, and pepper, stir, cover and cook on the Manual setting for 5 minutes. Release the pressure, uncover the Air fryer, and set it on Manual mode. Dash more salt and pepper, if desired, and the peas, stir, bring to a simmer, transfer to bowls, and serve hot.

Nutrition:

Calories: 230

Protein: 3 g.

Fat: 7 g.

Carbs: 10 g.

Chicken Noodle Soup

Preparation Time: 10 minutes

Cooking Time: 12 minutes

Servings: 6

Ingredients:

- 1 yellow onion, peeled and chopped
- 1 tablespoon butter
- 1 celery stalk, chopped
- 4carrots, peeled and sliced
- Salt and ground black pepper, to taste
- 6cups chicken stock
- cups chicken, already cooked and shredded
- Egg noodles, already cooked

Directions:

1. Put the air fryeron Sauté mode, add the butter and heat it up. Put in the onion, stir, and cook 2 minutes. Add the celery and carrots, stir, and cook 5 minutes. Add the chicken and stock, stir, cover the Air fryer and cook on the Soup setting for 5 minutes. Release the pressure, uncover the Air fryer, add salt and pepper to taste, and stir. Divide the noodles into soup bowls, add the soup over them, and serve.

Nutrition:

Calories: 100

Protein: 7 g.

Fat: 1 g.

Carbs: 4 g.

Zuppa Toscana

Preparation Time: 10 minutes

Cooking Time: 17 minutes

Servings: 8

Ingredients:

- 1 pound chicken sausage, ground
- 6bacon slices, chopped
- 3garlic cloves, peeled and minced
- 1 cup yellow onion, peeled and chopped
- 1 tablespoon butter
- 40ounces chicken stock
- Salt and ground black pepper, to taste
- Red pepper flakes
- 3potatoes, cubed
- 3tablespoons cornstarch
- 12ounces evaporated milk
- 1 cup Parmesan, shredded
- 2cup spinach, chopped

Directions:

1. Put the air fryeron Sauté mode, add the bacon, stir, cook until it's crispy, and transfer to a plate.
2. Add the sausage to the Air fryer, stir, cook until it browns on all sides, and also transfer to a plate.

3. Add the butter to the Air fryer and melt it. Put in the onion, stir, and cook for 5 minutes. Put in the garlic, stir, and cook for a minute. Pour in ⅓ of the stock, salt, pepper, and pepper flakes and stir. Place the potatoes in the steamer basket of the Air fryer, cover and cook on the Steam setting for 4 minutes. Release the pressure, uncover the Air fryer, and transfer the potatoes to a bowl. Add the rest of the stock to the Air fryer with the cornstarch mixed with the evaporated milk, stir, and Put the air fryeron Manual mode. Add the cheese, sausage, bacon, potatoes, spinach, more salt and pepper, if needed, stir, divide into bowls, and serve.

Nutrition:

Calories: 170

Protein: 10 g.

Fat: 4 g.

Carbs: 24 g.

Minestrone Soup

Preparation Time: 10 minutes

Cooking Time: 15 minutes

Servings: 8

Ingredients:

- 1 tablespoon extra virgin olive oil
- 1 celery stalk, chopped
- 2carrots, peeled and chopped
- 1 onion, peeled and chopped
- 1 cup corn kernels
- 1 zucchini, chopped
- 3pounds tomatoes, cored, peeled, and chopped
- 4garlic cloves, peeled and minced
- 29ounces chicken stock
- 1 cup uncooked pasta
- Salt and ground black pepper, to taste
- 1 teaspoon Italian seasoning
- 2cups baby spinach
- 15ounces canned kidney beans
- 1 cup Asiago cheese, grated
- 2tablespoons fresh basil, chopped

Directions:

1. Put the air fryeron Sauté mode, add the oil and heat it up. Put in the onion, stir, and cook for 5 minutes. Add the carrots, garlic, celery, corn, and zucchini, stir, and cook 5 minutes. Add the tomatoes, stock, Italian seasoning, pasta, salt, and pepper, stir, cover, and cook on the Soup setting for 4 minutes. Naturally release the pressure, uncover, add the beans, basil, and spinach. Dash more salt and pepper, if desired, divide into bowls, add the cheese on top, and serve.

Nutrition:

Calories –110

Protein: 5 g.

Fat: 2 g.

Carbs: 18 g.

Chicken and Wild Rice Soup

Preparation Time: 10 minutes

Cooking Time: 15 minutes

Servings: 6

Ingredients:

- 1 cup yellow onion, peeled and chopped
- tablespoons butter
- 1 cup celery, chopped
- 1 cup carrots, chopped
- 28ounces chicken stock
- 2chicken breasts, skinless, boneless and chopped

- 6ounces wild rice
- Red pepper flakes
- Salt and ground black pepper, to taste
- 1 tablespoon dried parsley
- 2tablespoons cornstarch
- 2tablespoons water
- 1 cup milk
- 1 cup half and half
- 4ounces cream cheese, cubed

Directions:

1. Put the air fryeron Sauté mode, add the butter and melt it. Add the carrot, onion, and celery, stir and cook for 5 minutes. Add the rice, chicken, stock, parsley, salt, and pepper, stir, cover, and cook on the Soup setting for 5 minutes. Release the pressure, uncover, add the cornstarch mixed with water, stir, and Put the air fryeron Manual mode. Add the cheese, milk, and half and half, stir, heat up, transfer to bowls, and serve.

Nutrition:

Calories: 200

Protein: 5 g.

Fat: 7 g.

Carbs: 19 g.

Creamy Tomato Soup

Preparation Time: 10 minutes

Cooking Time: 6 minutes

Servings: 8

Ingredients:

- 1 yellow onion, peeled and chopped
- 3tablespoons butter
- 1 carrot, peeled and chopped
- 2celery stalks, chopped
- 2garlic cloves, peeled and minced
- 29ounces chicken stock
- Salt and ground black pepper, to taste
- ¼ cup fresh basil, chopped
- 3pounds tomatoes, peeled, cored, and cut into quarters
- 1 tablespoon tomato paste
- 1 cup half and half
- ½ cup Parmesan cheese, shredded

Directions:

1. Put the air fryeron Sauté mode, add the butter and melt it. Mix in the onion, carrots, and celery, stir, and cook for 3 minutes.

2. Put in the garlic, stir, and cook for 1 minute. Put in the tomatoes, tomato paste, stock, basil, salt, and pepper, stir, cover, and cook on the Soup setting for 5 minutes.

3. Release the pressure, uncover the Air fryer and puree the soup using and immersion blender. Add the cheese and half and half, stir, Put the air fryeron Manual mode and heat everything up. Divide the soup into soup bowls, and serve.

Nutrition:

Calories: 280

Protein: 24 g.

Fat: 8 g.

Carbs: 32 g.

Tomato Soup

Preparation Time: 10 minutes

Cooking Time: 45 minutes

Servings: 6

Ingredients:

- For the roasted tomatoes:
- 14garlic cloves, peeled and crushed
- 3pounds cherry tomatoes, cut into halves
- Salt and ground black pepper, to taste
- 2tablespoons extra virgin olive oil
- ½ teaspoon red pepper flakes

For the soup:

1. 1 yellow onion, peeled and chopped
2. 2tablespoons olive oil
3. 1 red bell pepper, seeded and chopped

4. 3tablespoons tomato paste

5. 2celery ribs, chopped

6. 2cups chicken stock

7. 1 teaspoon garlic powder

8. 1 teaspoon onion powder

9. ½ tablespoon dried basil

10. ½ teaspoon red pepper flakes

11. Salt and ground black pepper, to taste

12. 1 cup heavy cream

For serving:

- Fresh basil leaves, chopped

- ½ cup Parmesan cheese, grated

Directions:

1. Take the tomatoes and garlic in a baking tray, drizzle 2 tablespoons oil, season with salt, pepper and a ½ teaspoon of red pepper flakes, toss to coat, introduce in the oven at 425°F, and roast for 25 minutes. Take the tomatoes out of the oven and set aside.

2. Put the air fryeron Sauté mode, add the oil, and heat it up. Add the onion, bell pepper, celery, salt, pepper, garlic powder, onion powder, basil, the remaining red pepper flakes, stir, and cook for 3 minutes.

3. Add the tomato paste, roasted tomatoes, and garlic and stir. Add the stock, cover the Air fryer, and cook on the Manual setting for 10 minutes. Release the pressure, uncover the Air fryer and set it on Sauté mode. Add the heavy cream and blend everything using an immersion blender. Divide in bowls, add basil and cheese on top, and serve.

Nutrition:

Calories: 150

Protein: 4 g.

Fat: 1 g.

Carbs: 3 g.

Carrot Soup

Preparation Time: 10 minutes

Cooking Time: 16 minutes

Servings: 4

Ingredients:

- 1 tablespoon vegetable oil
- 1 onion, peeled and chopped
- 1 tablespoon butter
- 1 garlic clove, peeled and minced
- 1 pound carrots, peeled and chopped
- 1 small ginger piece, peeled and grated
- Salt and ground black pepper, to taste
- ¼ teaspoon brown sugar
- 2cups chicken stock
- 1 tablespoon Sriracha
- 14ounces canned coconut milk
- Cilantro leaves, chopped, for serving

Directions:

1. Put the air fryeron Sauté mode, add the butter and oil, and heat them up. Put in the onion, stir and cook for 3 minutes.
2. Add the ginger and garlic, stir, and cook for 1 minute. Add the sugar, carrots, salt, and pepper, stir, and cook 2 minutes.

3. Add the sriracha, coconut milk, stock, stir, cover, and cook on the Soup setting for 6 minutes. Naturally release the pressure for 10 minutes, uncover the Air fryer, blend the soup with an immersion blender, add more salt and pepper, if needed, and divide into soup bowls. Add the cilantro on top, and serve.

Nutrition:

Calories: 60

Protein: 2 g.

Fat: 1 g.

Carbs: 12 g.

Cabbage Soup

Preparation Time: 10 minutes

Cooking Time: 10 minutes

Servings: 4

Ingredients:

- 1 cabbage head, chopped
- 12ounces baby carrots
- 3celery stalks, chopped
- ½ onion, peeled and chopped
- 1packet vegetable soup mix
- 2tablespoons olive oil
- 12ounces soy burger
- 3teaspoons garlic, peeled and minced
- ¼ cup cilantro, chopped
- 4cups chicken stock
- Salt and ground black pepper, to taste

Directions:

1. In the Air fryer, mix the cabbage with the celery, carrots, onion, soup mix, soy burger, stock, olive oil, and garlic, stir, cover, and cook on Soup mode for 5 minutes. Release the pressure, uncover the Air fryer, add the salt, pepper, and cilantro, stir again well, divide into soup bowls, and serve.

Nutrition:

Calories: 100

Protein: 10 g.

Fat: 1 g.

Carbs: 10 g.

Cream of Asparagus

Preparation Time: 10 minutes

Cooking Time: 25 minutes

Servings: 4

Ingredients:

- 2pounds green asparagus, trimmed, tips cut off and cut into medium pieces
- 3tablespoons butter
- 1yellow onion, peeled and chopped
- 6cups chicken stock
- ¼ teaspoon lemon juice
- ½ cup crème fraiche

- Salt and ground white pepper, to taste

Directions:

1. Put the air fryeron Sauté mode, add the butter and melt it. Add the asparagus, salt, and pepper, stir, and cook for 5 minutes. Add 5 cups of the stock, cover the Air fryer, and cook on Soup mode for 15 minutes. Release the pressure, uncover the Air fryer and transfer soup to a blender. Pulse several times and return to the Air fryer. Put the air fryeron Manual mode, add the crème fraiche, the rest of the stock, salt, pepper, and lemon juice, bring to a boil, divide into soup bowls, and serve.

Nutrition:

Calories: 80

Protein: 6.3 g.

Fat: 8 g.

Carbs: 16 g.

Veggie Noodle Soup

Preparation Time: 5 minutes

Cooking Time: 10 minutes

Servings: 4

Ingredients:

- Celery: 4 stalks, chopped into bite-sized pieces
- Carrots: 4, chopped into bite-sized pieces
- Sweet potatoes: 2, peeled and chopped
- Sweet onion: 1, chopped
- Broccoli florets: 1 cup
- Tomato: 1, diced
- Garlic: 2 cloves, minced
- Bay leaf: 1
- Dried oregano: 1 tsp.
- Dried thyme: 1 tsp.
- Dried basil: 1 tsp.
- Salt: 1 to 2 tsp.
- Ground black pepper
- Dried pasta: 1 cup
- Vegetable stock: 4 cups, plus more as needed
- Water: 1 to ½ cups, plus more as needed
- Chopped fresh parsley, for garnish
- Lemon zest for garnish
- Crackers, for serving

Directions:

1. In the Air fryer, combine the water, stock, pasta, salt, pepper, basil, thyme, oregano, bay leaf, garlic, tomato, broccoli, onion, sweet potatoes, carrots, and celery.
2. Cover the Air fryer.
3. Cook on High for 3 minutes.
4. Do a natural release and then a quick release.
5. Remove the lid and stir the soup.
6. Discard the bay leaf, garnish and serve.

Nutrition:

Calories: 120

Protein: 8 g.

Fat: 10 g.

Carbs: 22 g.

Carrot Ginger Soup

Preparation Time: 5 minutes

Cooking Time: 10 minutes

Servings: 2

Ingredients:

- Carrots: 7 chopped
- Fresh ginger: 1-inch, peeled and chopped
- Sweet onion: ½, chopped
- Vegetable stock: 1 ¼ cups
- Salt: ½ tsp.
- Sweet paprika: ½ tsp.
- Ground black pepper
- Cashew sour cream for garnish
- Fresh herbs for garnish

Directions:

1. In the Air fryer, combine the paprika, salt, stock, onion, ginger, and carrots. Season with pepper.
2. Cover the Air fryer.
3. Cook on High for 3 minutes.
4. Do a natural release and then a quick release.
5. Open and blend with a hand mixer until smooth.
6. Garnish and serve.

Nutrition:

Calories: 85

Protein: 6.7 g.

Fat: 8.5 g.

Carbs: 18 g.

Creamy Tomato Basil Soup

Preparation Time: 5 minutes

Cooking Time: 4 minutes

Servings: 4

Ingredients:

- Vegan butter: 2 Tbsp.
- Small sweet onion: 1, chopped
- Garlic: 2 cloves, minced
- Carrot: 1, chopped
- Celery: 1 stalk, chopped
- Vegetable stock: 3 cups
- Tomatoes: 3 pounds, quartered

- Fresh basil: ¼ cup, plus more for garnishing
- Nutritional yeast: ¼ cup
- Salt and ground black pepper
- Nondairy milk: ½ to 1 cup

Directions:

1. Press Sauté on the Air fryer, add butter and melt.
2. Put in the garlic and onion and stir-fry for 3 to 4 minutes.
3. Add celery and carrot and cook 2 minutes more. Stir continuously.
4. Add the stock and deglaze the pot.
5. Add salt, yeast, basil, and tomatoes. Stir to mix.
6. Cover the Air fryer.
7. Cook on High for 4 minutes.
8. Do a natural release than a quick release.
9. Open and blend with a hand mixer until smooth.
10. Stir in milk. Taste and adjust seasoning.
11. Garnish and serve.

Nutrition:

Calories: 70

Protein: 5.6 g.

Fat: 7.4g.

Carbs: 13 g.

Cream of Mushroom Soup

Preparation Time: 5 minutes

Cooking Time: 4 minutes

Servings: 4

Ingredients:

- Vegan butter: 2 Tbsp.
- Small sweet onion: 1, chopped
- White button mushrooms: 1 ½ pound, sliced
- Garlic: 2 cloves, minced
- Dried thyme: 2 tsp.
- Sea salt -1 tsp.
- Vegetable stock: 1 ¾ cup
- Silken tofu: ½ cup
- Chopped fresh thyme for garnishing

Directions:

1. Press Sauté on the Air fryer. Melt the butter and add the onion. Stir-fry for 2 minutes. Add the salt, dried thyme, garlic, and mushrooms. Stir-fry for 2 minutes more and press Cancel.
2. Stir in the stock. Cover the Air fryer.
3. Cook on High for 5 minutes.
4. Meanwhile, process the tofu in a food processor until smooth. Set aside.
5. Do a natural release, then quick release.
6. Open and blend with a hand mixer until smooth.

7. Garnish and serve.

Nutrition:

Calories: 80

Protein: 6.2 g.

Fat: 9 g.

Carbs: 17 g.

Chipotle Sweet Potato Chowder

Preparation Time: 3 minutes

Cooking Time: 2 minutes

Servings: 4

Ingredients:

- Vegetable stock: 1 ¼ cups
- Lite coconut milk: 1 (14-ounce) can
- Sweet potatoes: 2, peeled and diced
- Canned chipotle peppers: 2 to 4 (in adobo sauce), diced
- Red bell pepper: 1, diced
- Small onion: 1, diced
- Ground cumin: 1 tsp.
- Salt: ½ to 1 tsp.

- Frozen sweet corn: 1 ½ cups
- Adobo sauce from the canned peppers, to taste

Directions:

1. Whisk the coconut milk and stock in a bowl. Mix well.
2. Pour into the Air fryer. Add the salt, cumin, onion, bell pepper, chipotles, and sweet potatoes.
3. Cover the Air fryer.
4. Cook on High for 2 minutes.
5. Do a natural release, then quick release.
6. Remove the lid and add the adobo sauce and frozen corn.
7. Warn the corn and serve.

Nutrition:

Calories: 95

Protein: 8.5 g.

Fat: 9.2 g.

Carbs: 23 g.

Coconut Sweet Potato Stew

Preparation Time: 5 minutes

Cooking Time: 4 minutes

Servings: 4

Ingredients:

- Avocado oil: 2 Tbsp.
- Sweet onion: ½, diced
- Sweet potatoes: 2, peeled and cubed
- Garlic: 2 cloves, minced
- Salt: 1 to 1 ½ tsp.
- Ground turmeric: 1 tsp.
- Paprika: 1 tsp.
- Ground cumin: ½ tsp.
- Dried oregano: ½ tsp.
- Chili powder: 1 to 2 dashes
- Roma tomatoes: 2, chopped
- Lite coconut milk: 1 (14-ounce) can, shaken well
- Water: 1 ¼ cups, plus more as needed
- Chopped kale: 1 to 2 cups

Directions:

1. Choose Sauté on the Air fryer and add oil.
2. Add onion and stir-fry for 3 minutes.
3. Stir in chili powder, oregano, cumin, paprika, turmeric, salt, garlic, and sweet potatoes. Stir-fry for 1 minute.
4. Add the water, tomatoes, and coconut milk and mix.

5. Cover the Air fryer.

6. Cook on High for 4 minutes.

7. Do a natural release than a quick release.

8. Open and stir in the kale. Mix.

9. Serve.

Nutrition:

Calories: 105

Protein: 9.3 g.

Fat: 10 g.

Carbs: 25 g.

Italian Vegetable Stew

Preparation Time: 5 minutes

Cooking Time: 7 minutes

Servings: 4

Ingredients:

- Olive oil: 2 Tbsp.
- Leeks: 2, white and very light green parts only, chopped
- Sweet onion: 1, chopped
- Carrot: 1, chopped
- Celery: 1, sliced
- White mushrooms: 1 cup, sliced
- Small eggplant: 1, chopped
- Garlic: 3, cloves, minced
- Yukon gold potatoes: 3, chopped
- Roma tomatoes: 3, chopped
- Vegetable stock: 4 cups
- Dried oregano: 1 tsp.
- Salt: ½ tsp. plus more as needed
- Torn kale leaves: 2 cups
- Ground black pepper
- Fresh basil for garnishing

Directions:

1. Choose Sauté on the Air fryer and add oil.
2. Add eggplant, mushrooms, celery, carrot, onion, and leeks. Stir-fry for 2 minutes.

3. Add the garlic.

4. Cook 30 seconds more.

5. Add the salt, oregano, stock, tomatoes, and potatoes.

6. Cover the Air fryer.

7. Cook on High for 7 minutes.

8. Do a natural release and then a quick release.

9. Open and stir in the kale.

10. Taste and adjust seasoning.

11. Serve.

Nutrition:

Calories: 115

Protein: 10 g.

Fat: 12 g.

Carbs: 28 g.

Spinach Mint Stew

Preparation Time: 5 minutes

Cooking Time: 15 minutes

Servings: 4

Ingredients:

- 2cups heavy cream
- 1 tablespoon lemon juice
- 1 small onion, chopped
- 2cups fresh spinach, chopped
- 2garlic cloves, minced
- 1/2 teaspoon black pepper, (finely ground)
- 1 tablespoon mint leaves, torn
- 1 teaspoon salt
- 1 cup celery leaves, chopped
- 2tablespoon butter
- 1 cup celery stalks, chopped

Directions:

1. Arrange Air fryer over a dry platform in your kitchen. Open its top lid and switch it on.
2. Find and press "SAUTE" cooking function; add the butter in it and allow it to heat.
3. In the pot, add the onions, garlic, and celery stalks; cook (while stirring) until turns translucent and softened for around 2 minutes.

4. Add celery leaves and spinach; season to taste and stir-cook for 2-3 minutes.
5. Add in the heavy cream; gently stir to mix well.
6. Close top lid to create a locked chamber; make sure that safety valve is in locking position.
7. Find and press "MANUAL" cooking function; timer to 5 minutes with default "HIGH" pressure mode.
8. Allow the pressure to build to cook the ingredients.
9. After cooking time is over, press "CANCEL" setting. Find and press "QPR" cooking function. This setting is for quick release of inside pressure.
10. Slowly open the lid, stir in the mint and lemon juice. Take out the cooked recipe in serving plates or serving bowls and enjoy the keto recipe.

Nutrition:

Calories: 85

Protein: 7.1 g.

Fat: 8 g.

Carbs: 18.6 g.

Creamy Cauliflower and Sage Soup

Preparation Time: 10 minutes

Cooking Time: 10 minutes

Servings: 4

Ingredients:

- 1 teaspoon butter
- 1 large onion, chopped
- 4cloves garlic, minced
- 1 teaspoon ground sage
- 8cups cauliflower florets
- 3cups low-sodium chicken broth

- ½ teaspoon salt
- Pepper to taste
- ½ cup unsweetened coconut milk

Directions:

1. Select the Sauté setting and heat the butter. Mix in the onion and cook until clear, about 3-5 minutes. Add the garlic and sage and cook for 1 minute. Add the cauliflower, chicken broth, salt, and pepper, and stir well.

2. Press Cancel to reset the cooking Directions. Secure the lid and fix the Pressure Release to Sealing. Select the Pressure Cook or Manual setting and set the cooking time to 10 minutes at high pressure.

3. Once the timer is done, let sit for at least 10 minutes; the pressure will release naturally. Then switch the Pressure Release to Venting to allow any last steam out.

4. Open the lid and puree the soup using an immersion blender or by transferring it to a stand blender. Stir in the unsweetened coconut milk and add salt and pepper to taste.

Nutrition:

Calories: 171

Protein: 8.8 g.

Fat: 9.2 g.

Carbs: 18.1 g.

Curried Pumpkin Soup

Preparation Time: 10 minutes

Cooking Time: 5 minutes

Servings: 4

Ingredients:

- 2tablespoons butter
- 1 onion, chopped
- 2tablespoons curry powder
- 1/8 teaspoon cayenne pepper (optional)
- 4cups vegetable broth
- 4cups low-sodium pumpkin puree
- 1 tablespoon tamari
- Salt to taste
- Pepper to taste

  1½ cups unsweetened coconut milk

  1 teaspoon lemon juice

  Optional: ¼ cup roasted pumpkin seeds for serving

Directions:

1. Select the Sauté setting on the Air fryer and heat the butter. Add the onion and cook until translucent, 3-4 minutes.

2. Add the curry powder and cayenne (if using), and stir until fragrant 1-2 minutes. Pour in the vegetable broth and the cup of water. Stir in the pumpkin puree and tamari. Season to taste with salt and pepper.

3. Press Cancel to reset the cooking Directions. Secure the lid and fix the Pressure Release to Sealing. Select the Pressure Cook or Manual setting and set the cooking time to 5 minutes at high pressure.

4. Once done, set aside for at least 10 minutes; the pressure will release naturally. Then switch the Pressure Release to Venting to allow any last steam out.

5. Open the lid and puree the soup using an immersion blender or by transferring it to a stand blender. Stir in the unsweetened coconut milk and add salt and pepper to taste.

6. Ladle into bowls and top with roasted pumpkin seeds, if desired.

Nutrition:

Calories: 340

Protein: 5.8 g.

Fat: 24.9 g.

Carbs: 30.9 g.

My Signature Lemon Chicken Soup

Preparation Time: 10 minutes

Cooking Time: 6 minutes

Servings: 4

Ingredients:

- 1 tablespoon olive oil
- 1 medium onion, chopped
- 3cloves garlic, roughly chopped
- 2medium carrots, peeled and sliced
- 6stalks celery, sliced
- 8cups fat-free chicken broth
- 1 teaspoon dried thyme
- Salt to taste
- Pepper to taste
- 1½ lbs. boneless skinless chicken breasts
- 4oz. whole wheat spaghetti, broken in 1-inch pieces
- 1 bunch kale, stemmed and roughly chopped, to yield 1.5 cups
- 2lemons, juiced
- Optional: lemon wedges for serving

Directions:

1. Select the Sauté setting and heat the olive oil. Add the onion, garlic, carrots, and celery and sauté for 4-6 minutes.

2. Add the chicken broth and thyme. Add salt and pepper to taste. Add the chicken breasts and stir well.

3. Press Cancel to reset the cooking Directions. Secure the lid and fix the Pressure Release to Sealing. Select the Soup setting and set the cooking time to 6 minutes at high pressure.

4. Once done, set aside for at least 10 minutes; the pressure will release naturally. Then switch the Pressure Release to Venting to allow any last steam out.

5. Open the lid andtake out the chicken and shred. Add the broken spaghetti and stir; cook for time indicated on package. Add the chicken back to the pot and stir in the kale and lemon juice. Ladle into bowls and serve with an extra squeeze of lemon, drizzle of olive oil, or fresh cracked pepper.

Nutrition:

Calories: 388

Protein: 45 g.

Fat: 7 g.

Carbs: 35.1 g.

Fuss-Free French Onion Soup

Preparation Time: 5 minutes

Cooking Time: 20 minutes

Servings: 4

Ingredients:

- 3tablespoons unsalted butter
- 3large yellow onions, halved and then thinly sliced
- 2tablespoons balsamic vinegar
- 6cups beef broth
- 2large sprigs fresh thyme

  1 teaspoon salt

Directions:

1. Select the Sauté setting and heat the butter.

2. Add the onions and stir constantly until completely cooked down and caramelized. This can take 20-30 minutes or more, depending on your onions and the heat of your Air fryer. You're looking for a deep caramel color. If the onions begin to blacken at the edges, use the Adjust button to reduce the heat to Less.

3. Once the onions have caramelized, add the balsamic vinegar, red wine vinegar, broth, thyme, and salt, and scrape up any browned bits from the bottom of the pot.

4. Press Cancel to reset the cooking Directions. Secure the lid and fix the Pressure Release to Sealing. Select the Soup setting and set the cooking time to 10 minutes at high pressure.

5. Once done, set aside for at least 10 minutes; the pressure will release naturally. Then switch the Pressure Release to Venting to allow any last steam out.

6. Open the Air fryer and discard the thyme stems. Flavor with salt and pepper to taste and serve warm.

Nutrition:

Calories: 151

Protein: 5.5 g.

Fat: 9.4 g.

Carbs: 11.5 g.

Creamy Broccoli and Apple Soup

Preparation Time: 5 minutes

Cooking Time: 5 minutes

Servings: 4

Ingredients:

- 2tablespoons butter
- 3medium leeks, white parts only (frozen is fine!)
- 2shallots, chopped, about 3 tablespoons
- 1 large head broccoli, cut into florets
- 1 large apple, peeled, cored, and diced
- 4cups vegetable broth
- 1 cup unsweetened coconut milk
- Pepper to taste
- Salt to taste
- Optional: ¼ cup walnuts, toasted
- Optional: ¼ cup coconut cream

Directions:

1. Select the Sauté setting and heat the butter. Add the leeks and shallots and cook, stirring constantly, until softened, 4-6 minutes. Add the broccoli and apple and sauté another 5-6 minutes. Add the vegetable broth and stir well.

2. Press Cancel to reset the cooking Directions. Secure the lid and fix the Pressure Release to Sealing. Select the Pressure Cook or Manual setting and set the cooking time to 5 minutes at high pressure.

3. Once done, set aside for at least 10 minutes; the pressure will release naturally. Then switch the Pressure Release to Venting to allow any last steam out.

4. Open the lid and puree the soup using an immersion blender or by transferring it to a stand blender. Stir in the unsweetened coconut milk and add salt and pepper to taste.

5. Ladle into bowls and top with toasted walnuts or a drizzle of coconut cream.

Nutrition:

Calories: 259

Protein: 6.8 g.

Fat: 14.3 g.

Carbs: 32.3 g.

Immune-Boost Chard and Sweet Potato Stew

Preparation Time: 10 minutes
Cooking Time: 8 minutes
Servings: 2
Ingredients:

- 2tablespoons olive oil
- 1 tsp cumin seeds, or 1 tsp ground cumin
- 1 medium onion, diced
- 2medium sweet potatoes, peeled and in ½ inch cubes
- ½ teaspoon turmeric
- 1 tablespoon fresh ginger, peeled and minced
- 1 teaspoon salt
- 1 teaspoon ground coriander
- 2cups vegetable broth
- 1 bunch Swiss chard (about 12 oz)
- Optional: lemon wedges for serving

Directions:

1. Select the Sauté setting and heat the olive oil. Mix inthe onion and cook until clear, 3-5 minutes. If using cumin seeds, add them now and toast them for 1-3 minutes, until fragrant. Otherwise, add the ground cumin in the next step.

2. Add the sweet potato, ground cumin (if using), ginger, turmeric, coriander, and salt and cook for 3-4 minutes. Add the vegetable broth and chard. Add more salt and pepper if needed.

3. Press Cancel to reset the cooking Directions. Secure the lid and fix the Pressure Release to Sealing. Select the Pressure Cook or Manual setting and set the cooking time to 8 minutes at high pressure.

4. Once done, set aside for at least 10 minutes; the pressure will release naturally. Then switch the Pressure Release to Venting to allow any last steam out.

5. Scoop into bowls and serve warm with a squeeze of lemon juice, if desired.

Nutrition:

Calories: 308

Protein: 6.2 g.

Fat: 14.4 g.

Carbs: 42.6 g.

Moroccan Lentil Soup

Preparation Time: 10 minutes

Cooking Time: 10 minutes

Servings: 4

Ingredients:

- 1 tablespoon olive oil
- 1 small onion, chopped
- cloves garlic, minced
- 3/4 lb. ground turkey
- 1 tablespoon cumin
- 1 teaspoon garlic powder
- 1 teaspoon chili powder
- 1 teaspoon salt, plus more to taste
- ¼ teaspoon cinnamon
- Pepper to taste
- cups beef broth
- 1 cup green or brown lentils

Directions:

1. Select the Sauté setting and heat the olive oil. Put in the onion and garlic and sauté until fragrant, 2-3 minutes. Add the ground beef and cumin, garlic powder, chili powder, salt, cinnamon, and pepper. Cook until very well-browned and beginning to sear. Add the beef broth and scrape up any browned bits from the bottom of the pot. Add the lentils and stir well.

2. Press Cancel to reset the cooking Directions. Secure the lid and fix the Pressure Release to Sealing. Select the Soup setting and set the cooking time to 10 minutes at high pressure.
3. Once done, set aside for at least 10 minutes; the pressure will release naturally. Then switch the Pressure Release to Venting to allow any last steam out.
4. Open the Air fryer and taste; add more salt and pepper to taste. Ladle into bowls and serve with a drizzle of olive oil or fresh cracked pepper.

Nutrition:

Calories: 364

Protein: 31.3 g.

Fat: 12 g.

Carbs: 32.2 g.

Salmon Meatballs Soup

Preparation Time: 6 minutes

Cooking Time: 10 minutes

Servings: 5

Ingredients:

- 2cups hot water
- 2beaten large eggs
- 1 lb. ground salmon
- 2minced garlic cloves

- 2tbsps. butter

Directions:

1. In a bowl, mix butter, garlic, eggs and salmon. Apply a seasoning of pepper and salt.
2. Combine the mixture and use your hands to form small balls.
3. Place the fish balls in the freezer to set for 2 hours or until frozen.
4. Pour the hot water in the Air fryer and drop in the frozen fish balls.
5. Apply pepper and salt for seasoning.
6. Set lid in place and ensure vent is on "Sealing."
7. On "Manual" mode, set timer to 10 minutes.

Nutrition:

Calories: 199

Protein: 13.3 g.

Fat: 19.4 g.

Carbs: 0.6 g.

Turmeric Chicken Soup

Preparation Time: 6 minutes

Cooking Time: 15 minutes

Servings: 3

Ingredients:

- 1 bay leaf
- ½ cup coconut milk
- 2½ tsps. turmeric powder
- 4cups water
- 3boneless chicken breasts

Directions:

1. Place all ingredients in the Air fryer.
2. Give a good stir to mix everything.
3. Set lid in place and ensure vent points to "Sealing."
4. Set to "Poultry" mode and set timer to 15 minutes.
5. Do natural pressure release.

Nutrition:

Calories: 599

Protein: 46.8 g.

Fat: 61.4 g.

Carbs: 3.8 g.

Egg Drop Soup with Shredded Chicken

Preparation Time: 6 minutes

Cooking Time: 15 minutes

Servings: 6

Ingredients:

- 4beaten eggs
- cups shredded chicken
- 2tbsps. coconut oil
- 1 chopped celery
- 1 minced onion

Directions:

1. Choose the "Sauté" button on the Air fryer and heat the oil.
2. Sauté the onion and celery for 2 minutes or until fragrant.
3. Add the chicken and 4 cups water.
4. Apply pepper and salt for seasoning.
5. Set lid in place and ensure vent points to "Sealing."
6. Press the "Poultry" button and adjust the time to 10 minutes.
7. Do natural pressure release.
8. Once the lid is open, press the "Sauté" button and allow the soup to simmer.
9. Very gently, gradually pour in the beaten eggs and allow to simmer for 3 more minutes.

Nutrition:

Calories: 154

Protein: 9.6 g.

Fat: 12.8 g.

Carbs: 2.9 g.

Asian Egg Drop Soup

Preparation Time: 6 minutes

Cooking Time: 9 minutes

Servings: 3

Ingredients:

- 2beaten eggs
- 1 tsp. grated ginger
- 3cups water
- 2cups chopped kale
- 3tbsps. coconut oil

Directions:

1. Place all ingredients except for the beaten eggs in the Air fryer.

2. Apply pepper and salt for seasoning.

3. Set lid in place and ensure vent points to "Sealing."

4. On "Manual" mode, set timer to 6 minutes.

5. Do natural pressure release.

6. Once the lid is open, press the "Sauté" button and allow the soup to simmer.

7. Very gently, gradually pour in the beaten eggs and allow to simmer for 3 more minutes.

Nutrition:

Calories: 209

Protein: 6.5 g.

Fat: 20.3 g.

Carbs: 1.7 g.

30-Day Meal Plan

Day	Breakfast	Lunch/dinner	Dessert
1	Shrimp Skillet	Spinach Rolls	Matcha Crepe Cake
2	Coconut Yogurt with Chia Seeds	Goat Cheese Fold-Overs	Pumpkin Spices Mini Pies
3	Chia Pudding	Crepe Pie	Nut Bars
4	Egg Fat Bombs	Coconut Soup	Pound Cake
5	Morning "Grits"	Fish Tacos	Tortilla Chips with Cinnamon Recipe
6	Scotch Eggs	Cobb Salad	Granola Yogurt with Berries
7	Bacon Sandwich	Cheese Soup	Berry Sorbet
8	Noatmeal	Tuna Tartare	Coconut Berry Smoothie
9	Breakfast Bake with Meat	Clam Chowder	Coconut Milk Banana Smoothie

10	Breakfast Bagel	Asian Beef Salad	Mango Pineapple Smoothie
11	Egg and Vegetable Hash	Keto Carbonara	Raspberry Green Smoothie
12	Cowboy Skillet	Cauliflower Soup with Seeds	Loaded Berries Smoothie
13	Feta Quiche	Prosciutto-Wrapped Asparagus	Papaya Banana and Kale Smoothie
14	Bacon Pancakes	Stuffed Bell Peppers	Green Orange Smoothie
15	Waffles	Stuffed Eggplants with Goat Cheese	Double Berries Smoothie
16	Chocolate Shake	Korma Curry	Energizing Protein Bars
17	Eggs in Portobello Mushroom Hats	Zucchini Bars	Sweet and Nutty Brownies
18	Matcha Fat Bombs	Mushroom Soup	Keto Macho Nachos

19	Keto Smoothie Bowl	Stuffed Portobello Mushrooms	Peanut Butter Choco Banana Gelato with Mint
20	Salmon Omelet	Lettuce Salad	Cinnamon Peaches and Yogurt
21	Hash Brown	Onion Soup	Pear Mint Honey Popsicles
22	Black's Bangin' Casserole	Asparagus Salad	Orange and Peaches Smoothie
23	Bacon Cups	Cauliflower Tabbouleh	Coconut Spiced Apple Smoothie
24	Spinach Eggs and Cheese	Beef Salpicao	Sweet and Nutty Smoothie
25	Taco Wraps	Stuffed Artichoke	Ginger Berry Smoothie
26	Coffee Donuts	Spinach Rolls	Vegetarian Friendly Smoothie
27	Egg Baked Omelet	Goat Cheese Fold-Overs	ChocNut Smoothie
28	Ranch Risotto	Crepe Pie	Coco Strawberry Smoothie

			Egg Spinach
29	Scotch Eggs	Coconut Soup	Berries
			Smoothie
30	Fried Eggs	Fish Tacos	Creamy Dessert Smoothie

Conclusion

Thanks for making it to the end of this book. An air fryer is a relatively new addition to the kitchen, and it's easy to see why people are getting excited about using it. With an air fryer, you can make crispy fries, chicken wings, chicken breasts and steaks in minutes. There are many delicious foods that you can prepare without adding oil or grease to your meal. Again make sure to read the instructions on your air fryer and follow the rules for proper usage and maintenance. Once your air fryer is in good working condition, you can really get creative and start experimenting your way to healthy food that tastes great.

That's it! Thank you!

CPSIA information can be obtained
at www.ICGtesting.com
Printed in the USA
BVHW091203070521
606762BV00002B/127

9 781801 750530